Finance Act 2022

The impact on your exams

ACCA – Advanced Taxation (ATX – UK)

PREFACE

This booklet aims to provide a student-friendly summary of the key changes to UK tax rules introduced in the Finance Act 2022 (and associated changes made by other legislation).

It is a bespoke Finance Act summary, setting out the changes specifically for examination purposes.

It only includes changes with an impact on the ACCA Advanced Taxation (ATX-UK) examination syllabus for the June 2023 to March 2024 sittings.

Most temporary changes made during the COVID-19 pandemic, such as extension of some tax payment deadlines and changes to certain VAT rates, are excluded by ACCA from the syllabus. Those rule changes are therefore not in this booklet. Students should use only the normal tax rules, within the syllabus, for answers to the June 2023 to March 2024 examinations.

This booklet provides an easy way for students with prior knowledge of the ATX syllabus before FA2022 to update their knowledge with the latest relevant tax changes.

It is an ideal way for students to refresh their knowledge on key areas of change without having to purchase and read a completely new Study Text (which will incorporate latest changes but will not highlight where the changes are from previous studies).

This booklet also provides worked examples to illustrate the impact of the new provisions on examination-type calculations or questions.

This booklet is primarily aimed to help:

* those students retaking the ATX examination

* those who started studying under a previous Finance Act but have deferred their attempt to June 2023 or later, and

* those who have been successful at ATX but are interested in keeping their knowledge in key areas up to date and/or those who are considering continuing their professional qualification by taking the CIOT Chartered Tax Adviser examinations.

This is essential reading before attending the next study course for examinations to be taken in the sittings June 2023 to March 2024.

CONTENTS

NOTES

If you require a Study Text incorporating these changes, the FA2022 version of Kaplan Publishing's ATX learning materials is available. This has been produced primarily for use by students sitting the examination in the year April 2023 to March 2024 for the first time. Please go to www.kaplanpublishing.co.uk .

The chapter references given at the head of each section in Part B of this booklet enable easy cross reference to the relevant chapter of the FA2022 version of Kaplan ATX Study Text, but you do not need to have a copy of this version to benefit from this booklet.

INTRODUCTION

The ACCA are introducing a major change to the format of the ACCA ATX examinations sat in June 2023 to March 2024. More detail on the new examination format can be found in Part A of this booklet, along with further information on the CBE aspect.

There have been some changes to the content of the ATX syllabus, which are mainly due to the inclusions and exclusions of topics introduced in the Finance Act 2022. These are summarised in Part A; detailed information and examples of new areas are provided in Part B.

The ACCA have released information about the tax rates and allowances that will be provided in the June 2023 to March 2024 examination sittings. A full set of the tax rates and allowances, as they should appear in the examination, is given in Part C.

A   SYLLABUS AND EXAMINATION FORMAT CHANGES

1   INTRODUCTION

This section highlights the key changes in the syllabus and examination format that affect ATX-UK for the June 2023 to March 2024 sittings of the examination.

2   NEW TOPICS INCLUDED IN THE SYLLABUS

The major topics that have been added to the syllabus following FA2022 are:

- change in the balance of technical and professional skills marks (examination format)

- increase to the rate of income tax for dividend income (section 3.2)

- changes to thresholds and rates for national insurance contributions (section 6.2)

- increase to the rate of s455 tax for close companies (section 9.3)

3   TOPICS EXCLUDED FROM THE SYLLABUS

This is a list of changes made by FA2022, or by other legislation taking effect in the tax year 2022/23 or later, which the ACCA have confirmed are not in the ATX syllabus for the exams in June 2023 to March 2024:

- future increase in corporation tax rate from April 2023

- research and development relief for large companies

- minor changes to Real Estate Investment Trust rules

- implementation of VAT rules in free zones

- VAT exemption for dental prosthesis imports

- VAT relief for energy saving materials

- replacement of the VAT default surcharge regime from January 2023, and similar changes to late filing and payment penalties for other taxes.

- new HMRC powers for clamping down on promoters of tax avoidance

- new economic crime (Anti-money laundering) levy

- new rules for large businesses notification of uncertain tax treatments

- introduction of collective defined contribution (CDC) pension schemes

- transitional annual investment allowance rules in accounting periods which straddle the date of 1 April 2023

- tax exemption for household support fund payments

- new residential property developer tax (RPDT)

- reducing inheritance tax reporting requirements

Please note that you are not expected to make any reference to COVID-19 or the global economic crisis as a result of this pandemic in your exams. None of the temporary financial or legislative measures implemented as a result of COVID-19 are examinable.

4 EXAMINATION FORMAT

The new exam format will be as follows:

	Number of marks
Section A: 1 compulsory case-study question:	
Question 1	50

There will be 5 ethics marks and 10 professional skills marks in this section.

Section B: 2 compulsory 25 mark questions, covering both business and personal tax issues	
Question 1	25
Question 2	25

There will be 10 professional skills marks in this section
(5 professional skills marks for each question).

100

Total time allowed: 3 hours and 15 minutes.

Strategic Professional CBE

The ATX exam is now only available as a CBE.

This exam format may affect your approach to preparing to sit ATX. For example, in the Section A scenario-type exam questions, there will be marks available for using an appropriate format and style. When sitting the exam as a CBE you are able to choose the most appropriate answer method, either a word processor or a spreadsheet.

For more information regarding how to prepare for the CBE exam we advise that you make use of the ACCA Global website, which has a large number of resources (including a series of videos) about how to prepare to sit the ATX CBE.

You should also make use of the CBE practice software on the ACCA Practice Platform, including to practise exam-style questions from the Kaplan Exam Kit.

Professional skills marks

The ATX examination will consist of 80 technical marks and 20 professional skills marks. The following four key professional skills will be assessed in the ATX examination:

- communication
- analysis and evaluation
- scepticism
- commercial acumen

Professional skills marks are awarded to the overall question, rather than individual requirements.

Section A will examine all four professional skills.

Section B will examine a combination of analysis and evaluation, scepticism and commercial acumen.

For more information regarding professional skills we advise that you make use of the ACCA Global website, which has a series of videos explaining each professional skill.

B FINANCE ACT 2022

1 INTRODUCTION

This document highlights the key changes that affect the ATX examination for the June 2023 to March 2024 sittings of the examination due to the Finance Act 2022, or earlier legislation which took effect in tax year 2022/23 and Financial Year 2022.

2 TAX RATES AND ALLOWANCES

Tax rates and allowances can change each tax year. A copy of the tax rates and allowances for FA2022 given in the ATX examination, is reproduced in Part C of this booklet.

The rest of this booklet covers the effects of the rate changes and other legislative changes in FA2022.

It is broken down into the key tax areas as follows:

Section 3	Personal income tax
Section 4	Business income tax
Section 5	Pensions
Section 6	National insurance contributions
Section 7	Capital gains tax
Section 8	Inheritance tax
Section 9	Corporation tax
Section 10	Value added tax
Section 11	Stamp taxes
Section 12	Tax administration

3 PERSONAL INCOME TAX

3.1 Key changes

The key changes to personal income tax are covered as follows:

- income tax band limits and rates (section 3.2)

- income tax personal allowance (section 3.3)

- fixed amount of personal allowance transferable to spouse or civil partner (section 3.4)

- employment benefit rules (3.5)

3.2 Changes in income tax band limits and rates (Chapter 16)

3.2.1 Income tax rate increase for dividend income for 2022/23

In 2022/23 the income tax rates for non-savings and savings income are unchanged from 2021/22. So in summary:

- the basic rate of income tax continues to be 20%

- the basic rate band limit remains at £37,700

- the higher rate of income tax continues to be 40%

- the additional rate of tax continues to be 45%, and continues to apply where taxable income exceeds £150,000

When computing income tax liability, personal pension contributions and gift aid payments extend both the basic and higher rate bands by the gross contribution. It should be noted that gift aid donations are not in the ATX syllabus.

Illustration 1

Juanita has taxable income for the tax year 2022/23 of £160,000 that consists of £130,000 employment income and £30,000 property income. She makes personal pension contributions of £3,200 (net).

Juanita's income tax liability for the tax year 2022/23 is calculated as follows:

Juanita
Income tax computation – 2022/23

	Total	Non-savings income		
	£	£		
Taxable income **(Note)**	160,000	160,000		
Income tax:				
		£		£
Non-savings income (W)		41,700	× 20%	8,340
		112,300	× 40%	44,920
		154,000		
Non-savings income		6,000	× 45%	2,700
		160,000		
Income tax liability				55,960

Working: Extended band limits

	BR Band	HR Band
	£	£
Current band limit	37,700	150,000
Add: Gross PPCs (£3,200 × 100/80)	4,000	4,000
Revised band limit	41,700	154,000

Note: Juanita has a PA of £Nil as her ANI is >£125,140 – see section 3.3.2.

The income tax rates applying to dividend income in 2022/23 have been increased:

- falling in the basic rate band = 8.75%

- falling in the higher rate band = 33.75%

- falling in the additional rate band = 39.35%

The order of taxing income remains unchanged as follows:

- non-savings income (e.g. employment income, trading income, property income)

- then savings income

- then dividend income

3.3 The effect of the changes in income tax allowances (Chapter 16)

3.3.1 No change in the personal allowance

The personal allowance to use in the examination for the tax year 2022/23 is £12,570.

3.3.2 The reduction of the personal allowance for high income individuals

The personal allowance (PA) continues to be gradually reduced for individuals with income in excess of £100,000.

Where the taxpayer's adjusted net income (ANI) exceeds £100,000, the PA is reduced by:

$$50\% \times (ANI - £100,000)$$

If necessary, the reduced PA is rounded up to the nearest pound.

The ANI is calculated as follows:

	£
Net income	X
Less: Gross personal pension contributions	(X)
Adjusted net income (ANI)	X

A taxpayer with ANI in excess of £125,140 will therefore be entitled to no PA at all, as the excess income above £100,000 is more than twice the PA.

Remember that if there are any personal pension contributions, the gross amount will affect the ANI calculation and will also extend the basic and higher rate bands for the purposes of working out the rates of income tax payable on taxable income.

Method

- Calculate the individual's net income and ANI for the tax year 2022/23.

- Adjust PA if ANI exceeds £100,000 down to a minimum of £Nil.

- Calculate income tax on taxable income, remembering that the basic rate band normal limit (£37,700) and higher rate band normal limit (£150,000) are both extended by any gross personal pension contributions.

Illustration 2

Jimi received dividend income of £117,000 during the tax year 2022/23. He paid a personal pension contribution of £9,500. These amounts are stated gross.

Jimi's income tax liability is calculated as follows:

Jimi
Income tax computation – 2022/23

	£
Dividend income	117,000
Less: adjusted PA (W1)	(8,820)
Taxable income (all = dividend income)	108,180

Income tax:

£		£
2,000	× 0%	0
45,200	× 8.75% (W2)	3,955
60,980	× 33.75%	20,581
108,180		
Income tax liability		24,536

Workings

(W1) Adjusted PA

	£	£
PA		12,570
Net income (see note)	117,000	
Less: Gross PPC	(9,500)	
Adjusted net income	107,500	
Less: Income limit	(100,000)	
	7,500	
Reduction of PA (£7,500 × 50%)		(3,750)
Adjusted PA		8,820

Note: In this example, as there are no other sources of income and no reliefs, dividend income = total income = net income.

(W2) Extended band limits

	BR Band £	HR Band £
Current limit	37,700	150,000
Add: Gross PPC	9,500	9,500
Revised limit	47,200	159,500

Jimi's taxable income exceeds the basic rate limit/higher rate threshold but is below the threshold where the additional rate applies.

3.4   Transfer of personal allowance to spouse or civil partner (Chapter 16)

The optional election for a taxpayer to transfer a fixed amount of personal allowance (PA) to the taxpayer's spouse or civil partner remains available for the tax year 2022/23.

The conditions are unchanged from 2021/22 (so they are not repeated here).

3.4.1 The election

The election is to transfer a **fixed amount** of PA, regardless of actual unused PA, and is also referred to as the marriage allowance (MA). It is not possible to transfer more or less than the fixed amount.

Electing for the MA allows the transfer of £1,260 for the tax year 2022/23.

The figure of £1,260 is included in the tax rates and allowances provided to you in the examination, and is described there simply as the 'transferable amount'.

3.4.2 The effect of the election

The impact of this election on the two individuals' income tax computations is:

- the transferring spouse or civil partner's PA is reduced by the fixed amount (£1,260 in 2022/23)

- the recipient spouse's income tax liability is reduced by a maximum of £252 (being £1,260 MA × 20% BR income tax). If the recipient's income tax liability before applying this reduction is less than £252, no tax repayment is possible, but the amount by which the transferor's PA is reduced remains the full £1,260.

3.5   Changes to employment benefit rules (Chapter 17)

- Car and car fuel benefit (section 3.5.1)

- Van and van fuel benefit (section 3.5.2)

- No change in the official rate of interest (ORI) from 6 April 2021 (3.5.3)

3.5.1 Car and car fuel benefit

When calculating a car benefit, the relevant percentage still depends on the car's official CO_2 emissions.

In general, the car benefits percentages for tax year 2022/23 as provided in the tax tables are 1% higher than they were for tax year 2021/22, for the same CO_2 emissions.

The percentage for electric cars with zero CO_2 emissions is now 2%.

The percentages for electric-hybrid cars with emissions up to 50g/km depend upon its electric range, having identified this the relevant percentage can be found in the tax rates and allowances, an extract of which is shown below.

Electric range	Relevant %
130 miles or more	2
70 to 129 miles	5
40 to 69 miles	8
30 to 39 miles	12
Less than 30 miles	14

- For a car with emissions of between 51 to 54g/km the relevant percentage is 15%.

- The base level of emissions is 55g/km. The relevant percentage to use here is 16%. For every complete 5g/km that this figure is exceeded an additional 1% is added to this figure.

- An additional 4% continues to be added to the percentage for cars with a diesel engine. Cars that meet the RDE2 standard are still exempt from the diesel supplement.

- The maximum percentage that can be applied to any car has remained at 37%.

  Once calculated the relevant percentage is still applied to the list price of the car to calculate the benefit. A deduction can be made from the list price for capital contributions of up to £5,000.

  The car benefit is reduced by any contributions made by the employee towards running costs other than fuel.

- The fuel benefit continues to apply and is calculated when any private fuel is supplied to an employee for which the employee does not pay in full.

- The fuel benefit is not reduced by any contributions made by the employee towards fuel, but does not apply if the employee reimburses the employer in full for private fuel.

- The fuel benefit base figure has increased to £25,300, this is given in the tax rates and allowances.

- The percentage to use in the calculation of fuel benefit remains the same as that used to calculate car benefit.

Illustration 3

Middleton plc provides the following vehicles for use by employees in 2022/23:

Angus is provided with a petrol driven car with CO_2 emissions of 109g/km from 6 August 2022. The list price of the car was £22,000 but Angus contributed £3,000 towards its purchase. Angus is provided with fuel for business and private purposes costing £780. He pays the company £200 towards the cost of fuel.

Balbir is provided with an electric-hybrid car with CO_2 emissions of 26g/km on 6 April 2022. The car has an electric range of 39 miles. The car cost the company £14,000 although its list price was £15,200. Balbir has all his fuel paid by the company. He does not contribute anything towards running costs of the car.

Ceris is provided with a car throughout the tax year 2022/23, which she uses 50% privately. The car has CO_2 emissions of 102g/km and Ceris is reimbursed for all her diesel fuel costs. The car has a list price of £85,000 and does not meet the RDE2 standard.

The assessable car and fuel benefits for these employees are calculated as follows:

	£
Angus	
Car benefit (£19,000 (W1) × 26% (W2) × 8/12 (W3))	3,293
Fuel benefit (£25,300 × 26% (W2) × 8/12 (W3))	4,385
Total assessable benefits	7,678
Balbir	
Car benefit (£15,200 × 12%)(W4)	1,824
Fuel benefit (£25,300 × 12%)(W4)	3,036
Total assessable benefits	4,860
Ceris	
Car benefit (£85,000 × 29%) (W5)	24,650
Fuel benefit (£25,300 × 29%) (W5)	7,337
Total assessable benefits	31,987

Workings

(W1) A deduction can be made from the list price for capital contribution of up to £5,000. This reduces the list price used in the calculation of the car benefit to £19,000 (£22,000 – £3,000).

(W2) Appropriate percentage

	%
Basic % for petrol car	16
Plus: (105 – 55) ÷ 5	10
	26

The CO_2 emissions figure of 109 is rounded down to 105.

(W3) Reduction for non-availability

The car was available for eight months of 2022/23 so the car benefit and the fuel benefit are apportioned by 8/12.

Alternatively, the benefit can be calculated for the full year and reduced by 4/12.

(W4) The car is a hybrid with emissions not exceeding 50g/km therefore the relevant percentage depends on the electric range. This is between 30 to 39 miles meaning a percentage of 12%.

(W5) Appropriate percentage

	%
Basic % for petrol car	16
Plus: (100 – 55) ÷ 5	9
Plus: supplement for diesel car not meeting RDE2	4
	29

The CO_2 emissions figure of 102 is rounded down to 100.

3.5.2 Van and fuel benefit

The flat rate benefit for private use of a van (other than a zero emissions van) in 2022/23 has increased to £3,600 per annum. This benefit is not charged if private use of the van is 'insignificant'.

If the van provided has zero CO_2 emissions, then the benefit is exempt.

The annual scale charge for private use fuel provided for a company-owned van has increased to £688.

Both of the above rates are provided in the tax rates and allowances.

Electric vehicle charging facilities provided at or near the workplace do not count as a provision of fuel.

3.5.3 Living accommodation and beneficial loans – change in official rate of interest

The official rate of interest (ORI) from 6 April 2022 is unchanged 2%. This rate is provided in the tax rates and allowances. The following illustration reminds you how the ORI is used.

Illustration 4

Hussnan is provided with a house to live in by his employer throughout 2022/23. This accommodation is not job-related.

It cost his employer £160,000 in June 2018 and £40,000 was spent on improvements in December 2018. The house has an annual value of £4,000.

Hussnan is also provided with a loan of £18,000, at an annual interest of 1% by his employer, loaned to him 3 years ago. He has no other loans and has paid the employer interest only on a monthly basis.

Hussnan's taxable benefits for 2022/23 are:

	£
Accommodation	
Basic charge = annual value	4,000
Expensive accommodation	
(£160,000 + £40,000 − £75,000) × 2%	2,500
Loan	
£18,000 × (2% − 1%)	180
Total assessable benefits	6,680

4   BUSINESS INCOME TAX – No changes for the tax year 2022/23

4.1   There are no changes made by Finance Act 2022 to the business tax rules or allowances in the tax year 2022/23 compared with the previous tax year. The same information as for the previous year's exams will be given in the tax rates and allowances (see Part C of this booklet).

5   PENSIONS – No changes for the tax year 2022/23

5.1   There are no changes made by Finance Act 2022 to pensions tax rules or allowances in the tax year 2022/23 compared with the previous tax year. The same information as for the previous year's exams will be given in the tax rates and allowances (see Part C of this booklet).

6   NATIONAL INSURANCE CONTRIBUTIONS (NICs)

6.1   Key changes

The only changes to NICs rules within ATX syllabus for the tax year 2022/23 are to the various NIC limits and thresholds and NIC rates which are all given in the tax rates and allowances (see tables in Part C).

6.2   Changes to rates and allowances (Chapters 17 and 21)

The new limits and rates are set out in the tax rates and allowances in Part C of this update booklet. The main changes are set out below.

6.2.1 Class 1 employee

The earnings threshold for class 1 employees' NIC has increased to £12,570. This represents the point at which employees start to pay NIC on their cash earnings.

The upper earnings threshold for employee class 1 NIC remains at £50,270.

The rates of class 1 employee NIC have increased to 13.25% on earnings between £12,570 and £50,270, and 3.25% on earnings above £50,270.

6.2.2 Class 1 employer

The earnings threshold for class 1 employers' NIC has increased to £9,100. This represents the point at which employers start paying NIC on the employees earnings.

There continues to be no upper earnings threshold for employers class 1 NIC.

The rate of class 1 employer NIC has increased to 15.05%.

6.2.3 Class 1A

The rate of class 1A NIC has increased to 15.05%.

6.2.4 Class 2 NIC

The weekly rate for class 2 NIC has increased to £3.15 per week of trading.

The lower profits limit has increased to £12,570.

6.2.5 Class 4 NIC

For class 4 NIC the lower earnings threshold has increased to £12,570. This represents the point at which this class of NIC becomes payable.

The upper earnings threshold for class 4 NIC remains at £50,270. The rate of NIC payable reduces from this point.

The rates of class 4 NIC have increased to 10.25% on earnings between £12,570 and £50,270, and 3.25% on earnings above £50,270.

6.2.6 Employment allowance

The employment allowance (available to deduct from total employers' NIC for the tax year) has increased to £5,000 in 2022/23.

Illustration 5

Zaheer has a regularly paid salary of £52,220 throughout tax year 2022/23. He also receives employment benefits valued at £6,400.

The NIC liabilities of Zaheer and his employer on his total pay in 2022/23 are as follows:

Employee NIC	£
Employee's class 1 NIC	
Up to £12,570	0
(£50,270 – £12,570) × 13.25%	4,995
(£52,220 – £50,270) × 3.25%	63
	5,058

Employer's NIC	£
Employer's class 1 NIC	
Up to £9,100	0
(£52,220 – £9,100) × 15.05%	6,490
Class 1A NIC	
Benefits (£6,400 × 15.05%)	963
	7,453

Illustration 6

Praveen is self-employed, his tax adjusted profits for the tax year 2022/23 are £60,000.

His total NIC liability for the tax year 2022/23 is as follows:

Class 4 NIC	£
Up to £12,570	0
(£50,270 – £12,570) × 10.25%	3,864
(£60,000 – £50,270) × 3.25%	316
	4,180
Class 2 NIC	
(£3.15 × 52 weeks)	164

7 CAPITAL GAINS TAX (CGT)

7.1 Key changes

On disposal of a residential property the length of time to submit and pay the related tax has increased to 60 days.

All other CGT rates and allowances, all exemptions, reliefs, computational rules and tax payment rules (within the ATX syllabus) remain the same in the tax year 2022/23.

8 INHERITANCE TAX (IHT) – No changes for the tax year 2022/23

8.1 Key changes – none

No changes are made by FA2022 to any IHT rules.

The tax rates and allowances (see Part C) will now only give one nil rate band for IHT- which is £325,000.

9 CORPORATION TAX (CT)

9.1 Key changes

The rate of corporation tax for Financial Year 2022 is unchanged at 19%.

The changes to CT within the ATX exam syllabus, made by FA2022 (or by other legislation taking effect from April 2022), are as follows:

- Increase to the rate of s455 tax for close companies (section 9.3)

9.2 Enhanced capital allowances (Chapter 2)

The 130% super deduction and first year allowance at 50%, introduced in FA2021, continue to apply for companies in FA2022.

The tax treatment of the proceeds of later disposals of assets, which originally qualified for the super deduction, are not examinable in the ATX examinations in June 2023 to March 2024 so are not in this summary. Rules about accounting periods straddling 31 March 2023 are also not examinable.

9.3 Increase to the rate of s455 tax for close companies (Chapter 24)

The rate of s455 tax, which applies on the provision of loans to shareholders in a close company, has increased to 33.75%.

9.4 Research and development relief for large companies (Chapter 2)

Research and development relief for large companies has been removed from the ATX syllabus for examination sittings from June 2023 onwards.

Please note that research and development relief for small or medium sized enterprises (SMEs) is still examinable.

Illustration 7

Peacock Ltd has an accounting date of 31 March but changed this to 30 September in 2022 with a six-month accounting period ending 30 September 2022. At 1 April 2022 it had a main pool tax written down value (TWDV) of £Nil, and a special rate pool balance of £90,000.

In the six-month accounting period to 30 September 2022 the company spent £800,000 on new movable plant and machinery (no cars were included) and £1 million on new integral features incorporated into its factory building. There were no disposals in the period.

The maximum capital allowances for Peacock Ltd in the six months to 30 September 2022 are:

Period ended 30 September 2022	AIA	FYA	SRP	Allowances
	£	£	£	£
TWDV b/f			90,000	
Additions: With super deduction				
Plant and machinery £800,000 × 130%		1,040,000		
Super deduction at 130%		(1,040,000)		1,040,000
		————		
Additions: With AIA		0		
Integral features	1,000,000			
AIA (Max £1,000,000 × 6/12)	(500,000)			500,000
	————			
Balance of special rate pool expenditure for FYA	500,000	500,000		
WDA (6% × 6/12)			(2,700)	2,700
			————	
			87,300	
Additions: With FYA				
Enhanced FYA at 50%		(250,000)		250,000
		————		
Transfer to special rate pool			250,000	
			————	————
TWDV c/f/**Total allowances**			337,300	**1,792,700**
			————	————

Illustration 8

Saira is a shareholder in a close company, Moth Ltd. Moth Ltd prepares its accounts to 31 March annually and is not a large company for quarterly instalment purposes.

Moth Ltd loaned Saira £20,000 on 1 April 2022.

The tax implications for Moth Ltd in respect of the loan made to Saira are as follows.

Year ended 31 March 2023

Moth Ltd will suffer s455 tax of (£20,000 × 33.75%) £6,750.

The tax will be payable on 1 January 2024 (9 months and 1 day after the end of accounting period).

If any part of the loan is repaid before 1 January 2024 then the tax charge is reduced accordingly.

The £6,750 will be recoverable by Moth Ltd when the loan is repaid, or written off.

In addition to the above – if the loan is provided to Saira at a beneficial interest rate (below the official rate of interest of 2%), there will be a taxable benefit in kind for Saira (section 3.5.3).

Saira would be subject to an income tax charge, and Moth Ltd would be subject to class 1A NIC on the value of the benefit.

---

10 INDIRECT TAX

10.1 Key changes (Chapter 27)

From 1 April 2022 all VAT registered businesses will be required to use making tax digital (MTD), whether or not their turnover exceeds the registration threshold.

No other changes, within ACCA ATX syllabus, are made by FA2022 to the VAT rules for the tax year 2022/23.

11 TAX ADMINISTRATION

11.1 Key changes

There are very few syllabus changes this year affecting tax administration. The changes which do apply are covered as follows:

- Increase in the rate of interest charged on underpaid tax (section 11.3).

11.2 Update of the key due dates in the ATX syllabus

A summary of the key due dates for making elections and claims for the tax year 2022/23 is given in Appendix 4.

11.3 The interest rates to use in the examination (Chapters 1, 15 and 27)

The rate of interest on underpaid tax ('late payment interest') for use in the ATX examination has increased to 3.25%.

The rate of interest on overpaid tax ('repayment interest') for use in the ATX examination remains unchanged at 0.5%.

These figures are both given in your tax rates and allowances.

C   TAX RATES AND ALLOWANCES

The tax rates and allowances below will be reproduced in the examination for ATX for the June 2023 to March 2024 sittings.

SUPPLEMENTARY INSTRUCTIONS

1   You should assume that the tax rates and allowances for the tax year 2022/23 and for the financial year to 31 March 2023 will continue to apply for the foreseeable future unless you are instructed otherwise.

2   Calculations and workings need only be made to the nearest £.

3   All apportionments should be made to the nearest month.

4   All workings should be shown.

Income tax

		Normal rates	Dividend rates
Basic rate	£1 – £37,700	20%	8.75%
Higher rate	£37,701 – £150,000	40%	33.75%
Additional rate	£150,001 and over	45%	39.35%
Savings income nil rate band	– Basic rate taxpayers		£1,000
	– Higher rate taxpayers		£500
Dividend nil rate band			£2,000

A starting rate of 0% applies to savings income where it falls within the first £5,000 of taxable income.

Personal allowance

Personal allowance	£12,570
Transferable amount	£1,260
Income limit	£100,000

Where adjusted net income is £125,140 or more, the personal allowance is reduced to zero

Residence status

Days in UK	Previously resident	Not previously resident
Less than 16	Automatically not resident	Automatically not resident
16 to 45	Resident if 4 UK ties (or more)	Automatically not resident
46 to 90	Resident if 3 UK ties (or more)	Resident if 4 UK ties
91 to 120	Resident if 2 UK ties (or more)	Resident if 3 UK ties (or more)
121 to 182	Resident if 1 UK tie (or more)	Resident if 2 UK ties (or more)
183 or more	Automatically resident	Automatically resident

Remittance basis charge

UK resident for:	Charge
Seven out of the last nine years	£30,000
12 out of the last 14 years	£60,000

Car benefit percentage

The relevant base level of CO_2 emissions is 55 grams per kilometre.

The percentage rates applying to petrol cars (and diesel cars meeting the RDE2 standard) with CO_2 emissions up to this level are:

51 grams to 54 grams per kilometre	15%
55 grams per kilometre	16%

The percentage for electric cars with zero CO_2 emissions is 2%.

For hybrid-electric cars with CO_2 emissions between 1 and 50 grams per kilometre, the electric range of the car is relevant:

Electric range

130 miles or more	2%
70 to 129 miles	5%
40 to 69 miles	8%
30 to 39 miles	12%
Less than 30 miles	14%

Car fuel benefit

The base figure for calculating the car fuel benefit is £25,300.

Company van benefits

The company van benefit scale charge is £3,600, and the van fuel benefit is £688.

Vans producing zero emissions have a 0% benefit.

Individual savings accounts (ISAs)

The overall investment limit is £20,000.

Rent a room relief

The rent a room relief limit is £7,500.

Pension scheme limits

Annual allowance	£40,000
Minimum allowance	£4,000
Threshold income limit	£200,000
Income limit	£240,000
Lifetime allowance	£1,073,100

The maximum contribution that can qualify for tax relief without any earnings is £3,600.

Approved mileage allowances: cars

Up to 10,000 miles	45p
Over 10,000 miles	25p

Capital allowances: rates of allowance

Plant and machinery

Main pool	18%
Special rate pool	6%

Cars

New cars with zero CO_2 emissions	100%
CO_2 emissions between 1 and 50 grams per kilometre	18%
CO_2 emissions over 50 grams per kilometre	6%

Annual investment allowance

Rate of allowance	100%
Expenditure limit	£1,000,000

Enhanced capital allowances for companies

Main pool super deduction	130%
Special rate pool first year allowance	50%

Structures and buildings allowance

Straight line allowance	3%

Cash basis accounting

Revenue limit	£150,000

Cap on income tax reliefs

Unless otherwise restricted, reliefs are capped at the higher of £50,000 or 25% of income.

Corporation tax

Rate of tax	– Financial year 2022	19%
	– Financial year 2021	19%
	– Financial year 2020	19%
Profit threshold		£1,500,000

Value added tax (VAT)

Standard rate	20%
Registration limit	£85,000
Deregistration limit	£83,000

Inheritance tax

Nil rate band	£325,000
Residence nil rate band	£175,000

Rate of tax on excess over nil rate band	– Lifetime rate	20%
	– Death rate	40%

Inheritance tax: taper relief

Years before death	Percentage reduction
More than 3 but less than 4 years	20%
More than 4 but less than 5 years	40%
More than 5 but less than 6 years	60%
More than 6 but less than 7 years	80%

Capital gains tax: tax rates

	Normal rates	Residential property
Lower rate	10%	18%
Higher rate	20%	28%
Annual exempt amount		£12,300

Capital gains tax: business asset disposal relief and investors' relief

Lifetime limit – business asset disposal relief	£1,000,000
– investors' relief	£10,000,000
Rate of tax	10%

National insurance contributions

Class 1 Employee	£1 – £12,570 per year	Nil
	£12,571 – £50,270 per year	13.25%
	£50,271 and above per year	3.25%
Class 1 Employer	£1 – £9,100 per year	Nil
	£9,101 and above per year	15.05%
	Employment allowance	£5,000
Class 1A		15.05%
Class 2	£3.15 per week	
	Lower profits limit	£12,570
Class 4	£1 – £12,570 per year	Nil
	£12,570 – £50,270 per year	10.25%
	£50,271 and above per year	3.25%

Rates of interest(assumed)

Official rate of interest	2.00%
Rate of interest on underpaid tax	3.25%
Rate of interest on overpaid tax	0.50%

Standard penalties for errors

Taxpayer behaviour	Maximum penalty	Minimum penalty – unprompted disclosure	Minimum penalty – prompted disclosure
Deliberate and concealed	100%	30%	50%
Deliberate but not concealed	70%	20%	35%
Careless	30%	0%	15%

Stamp duty land tax on non-residential properties

Up to £150,000	0%
£150,001 – £250,000	2%
£250,001 and above	5%

Stamp duty

Shares	0.5%

APPENDICES

Appendix 1: Pro forma capital allowances computation – unincorporated businesses

	Notes	£	Main pool £	Special rate pool £	Short life asset £	Private use asset (Note 2) £	Allowances £
TWDV b/f			X	X	X		
Additions:							
Not qualifying for AIA or FYA:							
Second-hand zero emission cars	(1)						
Cars (1g/km to 50g/km)			X				
Cars (>50g/km)			X	X			
Car with private use				X		X	
Qualifying for AIA:							
Special rate pool expenditure	(3)	X					
AIA (Max £1,000,000 in total)		(X)					X
Transfer balance to special rate pool				X			
Plant and machinery		X					
AIA (Max £1,000,000 in total)		(X)					X
Transfer balance to main pool			X				
Disposals (lower of original cost or sale proceeds)	(4)		(X)		(X)		
			X	X	X	X	
BA/(BC)			X	X	X/(X)	X	X/(X)
Small pools WDA (if applicable)	(5)				NIL		
WDA at 18%			(X)				X
WDA at 6%				(X)			X
WDA at 6%/18% (depending on emissions)						(X) × BU%=	X
Additions qualifying for FYAs:							
New zero emission cars		X					
FYA at 100%		(X)	0				X
TWDV c/f			X	X		X	
Total allowances							X

Notes to the pro forma capital allowances computation

(1)   Cars are pooled according to their CO_2 emissions into either the main pool or special rate pool.

New zero emission cars receive 100% FYA.

(2)   Cars with private use are de pooled regardless of their CO_2 emissions and only the business proportion of allowances can be claimed.

However, the CO_2 emissions are important in determining the rate of WDA available.

(3)   Allocate the AIA to the special rate pool expenditure in priority to plant and machinery assets as a WDA of only 6% is available on the special rate pool as opposed to 18% available on main pool items.

(4)   Expenditure qualifying for AIA in the main pool which exceeds the level of AIA available is eligible for a WDA of 18%.

(5)   Small pools WDA: can claim up to a maximum WDA of £1,000 but on the main pool and/or special rate pool only.

(6)   The taxpayer does not have to claim all or any of the AIA or WDA.

Appendix 2: Pro forma capital allowances computation – companies

Description	Notes	AIA £	FYA £	Main pool £	Special rate pool £	Short life asset £	Allowances £
TWDV b/f	(1)			X	X	X	
Additions:							
Not qualifying for AIA or FYA:							
Second-hand zero emission cars				X			
Cars (1g/km to 50g/km)				X			
Cars (>50g/km)					X		
Qualifying for super deduction:							
Plant and machinery acquired on/after 1.4.21 (X × 130%)	(2)		X				
Super deduction at 130%			(X)				X
			0				
Qualifying for AIA:							
Special rate pool expenditure (pre 1.4.21)	(3)	X					
AIA (Max £1,000,000 in total)		(X)					
Transfer balance to special rate pool					X		
Main pool expenditure (second-hand/pre 1.4.21)		X					
AIA (Max £1,000,000 in total)		(X)					
Transfer balance to main pool	(4)			X			
Special rate pool expenditure (on/after 1.4.21)		X					
AIA (Max £1,000,000 in total)		(X)					
Balance of special rate pool expenditure for FYA			X				X
Disposals (lower of original cost or sale proceeds)				(X)		(X)	
BA/(BC)				X	X	X X/(X)	X/(X)
Small pools WDA (if applicable)	(5)					NIL	
WDA at 18%				(X)			X
WDA at 6%					(X)		X
WDA at 6%/18% (depending on emissions)							X

Additions qualifying for FYAs:

Enhanced FYA at 50% on balance of special rate pool expenditure	(6)	(X)		X
New zero emission cars		X		
FYA at 100%		(X)		
TWDV c/f			0	
			X	X
Total allowances				X

Notes to the pro forma capital allowances computation

(1) Cars are pooled according to their CO_2 emissions into either the main pool or special rate pool.

New zero emission cars receive 100% FYA.

(2) New main pool assets (other than cars) purchased between 1 April 2021 and 31 March 2023 qualify for the 130% super deduction.

(3) Allocate the AIA to the special rate pool expenditure in priority to plant and machinery assets as a WDA of only 6% is available on the special rate pool as opposed to 18% available on main pool items.

(4) Expenditure qualifying for AIA in the main pool which exceeds the level of AIA available is eligible for a WDA of 18%.

(5) Small pools WDA: can claim up to a maximum WDA of £1,000 but on the main pool and/or special rate pool only.

(6) New special rate pool assets (other than cars) purchased between 1 April 2021 and 31 March 2023 qualify for the 50% first year allowance. The balance goes to the special rate pool but does not qualify for WDA until the following accounting period.

(7) The taxpayer does not have to claim all or any of the AIA or WDA.

Appendix 3

Capital allowance illustrations

Illustration 1

Lapse Ltd runs a manufacturing business and has always prepared its accounts to 30 November each year, but changed its accounting date in 2022.

During the eleven months ending 31 October 2022 Lapse Ltd incurred the following expenditure:

1 December 2021	Purchased a second-hand machine for £26,000. This is expected to last seven years and be worthless at the end of its life. The short life asset election is made.
1 January 2022	Spent £923,334 on a second-hand air-conditioning system for the factory building which is expected to last 20 years.
1 May 2022	Purchased a new fully-electric car for £27,000. This has zero emissions and is to be used by the production manager. Private use will be 25%.
1 July 2022	Spent £90,000 on a new lorry.
15 July 2022	Purchased a new car for £18,000 which will be used by the managing director. CO_2 emissions are 75 g/km and private use will be 20%.
5 August 2022	Purchased a new lift for the office building for £300,000.

In addition, on 1 July 2022 the company sold an old machine for £10,000 (original cost £15,000).

As at 1 December 2021 the tax written down values were as follows:

Main pool	£73,000
Special rate pool	£90,000

Lapse Ltd's capital allowances computation would be calculated as follows:

	AIA	FYA	Main Pool	Special rate pool	Short life Asset	Allowances
	£	£	£	£	£	£
TWDV b/f			73,000	90,000		
Additions:						
No AIA/FYA						
Car – emissions exceeding 50 g/km				18,000		
Additions: With super deduction						
Lorry (£90,000 × 130%)		117,000				
Super deduction at 130%		(117,000)				117,000
Additions: With AIA		0				
Air conditioning (second-hand)	923,334					
AIA (Max £1,000,000 × 11/12) (Note)	(916,667)					916,667
Transfer balance to special rate pool				6,667		
Lift	300,000					
AIA (Max £1,000,000 × 11/12) (Note)	(0)					
Balance of special rate pool expenditure for FYA		300,000				
Machine	26,000					
AIA (Max £1,000,000 × 11/12) (Note)	(0)					0
Transfer balance to short life asset					26,000	
Disposal (lower of cost or sale proceeds)			(10,000)			
			63,000	114,667		
WDA (18% × 11/12)			(10,395)		(4,290)	14,685
WDA (6% × 11/12)				(6,307)		6,307
Additions: With FYA						
Enhanced FYA at 50% on balance of SRP expenditure		(150,000)				150,000
				150,000		
New Car – zero emissions	27,000					
FYA at 100%	(27,000)					27,000
			0			
TWDV c/f			52,605	258,360	21,710	
Total allowances						1,231,659

Notes: Super deduction is not available on the £26,000 machine and neither is the special rate pool FYA available on the air conditioning, this is because they are second-hand purchases.

The lorry is eligible for 130% super deduction as it was purchased new after 1 April 2021. This should be given in preference to AIA since it gives greater relief.

The AIA is allocated to the additions in the special rate pool (WDA 6%) in priority to the additions in the main pool (WDA 18%).

As the period is only 11 months, the AIA and WDA must be time apportioned. However, the FYA is never time apportioned.

There are no private use adjustments for companies; permitted private use of assets by company staff or directors is still business use by the company.

The new lift qualifies for 50% FYA but the balance is not eligible for WDA until the following accounting period.

Illustration 2

Jellena is in business as a sole trader and prepares accounts to 31 December each year.

During the year ending 31 December 2022 she incurred the following expenditure:

15 May 2022	Purchased new office furniture for £18,800.
2 June 2022	Purchased a new car with emissions of 90g/km for £26,667. Jellena will use the new car 20% of the time for private purposes.
10 June 2022	Installed a new water heating system in her business premises at a cost of £75,000 and a new lighting system at a cost of £8,000.

In addition, on 1 July 2022 she sold office equipment for £2,200 (original cost £11,000).

As at 1 January 2022 the tax written down values were as follows:

Main pool	£3,000
Short life asset	£9,000

Jellena's capital allowances computation would be calculated as follows:

Jellena
Capital allowances computation for the year ending 31 December 2022

	£	Main pool £	Special rate pool £	Short life asset £	Private use asset £	B.U.%	Allowances £
TWDV b/f		3,000	–	9,000			
Additions:							
No AIA/FYA							
Car – emissions > 50 g/km					26,667		
Qualifying for AIA:							
Water heating and lighting systems	83,000						
AIA (Max £1,000,000) (Note)	(83,000)						83,000
			0				
Plant and machinery							
Furniture	18,800						
AIA (Max £1,000,000) (Note)	(18,800)						18,800
Disposal proceeds							
(lower of cost or sale proceeds)		(2,200)					
		800	0	9,000	26,667		
Small pool WDA		(800)					800
WDA at 18%				(1,620)			1,620
WDA at 6%					(1,600)	× 80%	1,280
TWDV c/f		0	0	7,380	25,067		
Total allowances							105,500

Note: The AIA is allocated to the additions in the special rate pool (WDA 6%) in priority to the additions in the main pool (WDA 18%) but the order makes no difference here as the AIA is sufficient to cover all qualifying additions.

Appendix 4

Time limits for elections and claims

Income tax

Election/claim	Time limit	For 2022/23
Agree the amount of trading losses to carry forward	4 years from the end of the tax year in which the loss arose	5 April 2027
Current and prior year set-off of trading losses against total income	12 months from 31 January following the end of the tax year in which the loss arose	31 January 2025
Current and prior year set-off of trading losses against capital gains	12 months from 31 January following the end of the tax year in which the loss arose	31 January 2025
Three year carry back of trading losses in the opening years	12 months from 31 January following the end of the tax year in which the loss arose	31 January 2025
Three year carry back of terminal trading losses in the closing years	4 years from the end of the last tax year of trading	5 April 2027
Set-off of loss on the disposal of unquoted trading company shares against income	12 months from 31 January following the end of the tax year in which the loss arose	31 January 2025
Transfer of assets eligible for capital allowances between connected parties at TWDV	2 years from the date of sale	

Capital gains tax

Election/claim	Time limit	For 2022/23
Replacement of business asset relief for individuals (Rollover relief)	4 years from the end of the tax year in which the: – disposal is made, or – replacement asset is acquired whichever is later	5 April 2027 for 2022/23 sale or acquisition (if later event)
Holdover relief of gain on the gift of a business asset (Gift holdover relief)	4 years from the end of the tax year in which the disposal occurred	5 April 2027
Disapplication of incorporation relief	2 years from the 31 January following the end of the tax year in which the business is transferred If sell all shares by 5 April following tax year of incorporation: (Time limit 12 months earlier than normal latest claim)	31 January 2026 31 January 2025
EIS reinvestment relief	5 years from 31 January following the end of the tax year in which the disposal occurred	31 January 2029
Business asset disposal relief	12 months from 31 January following the end of the tax year in which the disposal occurred	31 January 2025
Determination of private residence	2 years from the acquisition of the second property	

Self-assessment – individuals

Election/claim	Time limit	For 2022/23
Pay days for income tax and class 4 NIC	1st instalment: 31 January in the tax year	31 January 2023
	2nd instalment: 31 July following the end of the tax year	31 July 2023
	Balancing payment: 31 January following the end of the tax year	31 January 2024
Pay day for CGT on UK residential property disposals	Within 60 days of the disposal	
Pay day for other CGT and class 2 NIC	31 January following the end of the tax year	31 January 2024
Filing dates If notice to file issued by 31 October following end of tax year	Paper return: 31 October following end of tax year	31 October 2023
	Electronic return: 31 January following end of tax year	31 January 2024
If notice to file issued after 31 October following end of tax year	3 months from the date of issue of the notice to file	
Retention of records – Business records	5 years from 31 January following the end of the tax year	31 January 2029
– Personal records	12 months from 31 January following the end of the tax year	31 January 2025
HMRC right of repair (i.e. to correct mistakes)	9 months from the date the return was filed	
Taxpayers right to amend a return	12 months from 31 January following the end of the tax year	31 January 2025
Taxpayers claim for overpayment relief	4 years from the end of the tax year	5 April 2027
HMRC can open a compliance check	12 months from the actual submission of the return	

Election/claim	Time limit	For 2022/23
HMRC can raise a discovery assessment		
– No careless or deliberate behaviour	4 years from the end of the tax year	5 April 2027
– Tax lost due to careless behaviour	6 years from the end of the tax year	5 April 2029
– Tax lost due to deliberate behaviour	20 years from the end of the tax year	5 April 2043
Taxpayers right of appeal against an assessment	30 days from the assessment – appeal in writing	

National Insurance Contributions

Election/claim	Time limit	For 2022/23
Class 1 employees' and employers' – pay days	17 days after the end of each tax month under PAYE system (14 days if not paid electronically)	22nd of each month
Class 1 A NIC – pay day	22 July following end of tax year (19 July if not paid electronically)	22 July 2023
Class 2 NICs – pay day	Paid under self-assessment with balancing payment and CGT liability	31 January 2024
Class 4 NICs – pay days	Paid under self-assessment with income tax – within POAs and balancing payment	In POAs, and then 31 January 2024

Corporation tax

Election/claim	Time limit
Replacement of business asset relief for companies (Rollover relief)	4 years from the end of the accounting period: – in which the disposal occurred or – the replacement asset was acquired whichever is later
Set-off of brought forward losses against total profits (income and gains)	2 years from the end of the accounting period in which the loss is relieved
Current year set-off of trading losses against total profits (income and gains) and 12 month carry back of trading losses against total profits (income and gains)	2 years from the end of the accounting period in which the loss arose
Surrender of current period trading losses to other group companies (Group relief and consortium relief)	2 years after the claimant company's accounting period
Election for transfer of capital gain or loss to another company within the gains group	2 years from the end of the accounting period in which the disposal occurred by the company actually making the disposal

Self-assessment – companies

Election/claim	Time limit
Pay day for small and medium companies	9 months and one day after the end of the accounting period
Pay day for large companies	Instalments due on 14th day of: – Seventh – Tenth – Thirteenth, and – Sixteenth month **after the start** of the accounting period
Filing dates	Later of: – 12 months from the end of the accounting period – 3 months from the issue of a notice to deliver a corporation tax return
HMRC right of repair (i.e. to correct mistakes)	9 months from the date the return was filed
Company's right to amend a return	12 months from the filing date

Election/claim	Time limit
Companies claim for overpayment relief	4 years from the end of the accounting period
HMRC can open a compliance check	12 months from the actual submission of the return
Retention of records	6 years from the end of the accounting period

Value added tax

Election/claim	Time limit
Compulsory registration	
– Historic test: Notify HMRC Charge VAT	– 30 days from end of the month in which the threshold was exceeded – First day of the second month after the taxable supplies exceeded the threshold
– Future test: Notify HMRC Charge VAT	– 30 days from the date it is anticipated that the threshold will be exceeded – The date it is anticipated that the threshold will be exceeded (i.e. the beginning of the 30 day period)
Compulsory deregistration	30 days from cessation
Filing of VAT return and payment of VAT	One month and seven days after the end of the return period

Inheritance tax

Election/claim	Time limit	For 2022/23
Lifetime IHT on CLTs – pay day	Gift before 1 October in tax year – following 30 April Gift on/after 1 October in tax year – 6 months after the end of the month of the gift	30 April 2023
Death IHT on lifetime gifts within 7 years of death (CLTs and PETs)	6 months after the end of the month of death	
IHT on estate	6 months after the end of the month of death	
Transfer of unused nil rate band to spouse or civil partner	2 years from the date of the second death	